The Fair Penitent by Nicholas Rowe

Adapted from *The Fatal Dowry* by Nathan Field & Philip Massinger

Nicholas Rowe was born in Little Barford, Bedfordshire, England, on June 20th, 1674.

He was educated at Highgate School, and then at Westminster School under the tutelage of Dr. Busby.

In 1688, Rowe became a King's Scholar, and then in 1691 gained entrance into Middle Temple. This was his father's decision (he was a barrister) who felt that his son had made sufficient progress to study law. While at Middle Temple, he decided that studying law was easier if seen as a system of rational government and impartial justice and not as a series of precedents, or collection of positive precepts.

On his father's death, when he was nineteen, he became the master of a large estate and an independent fortune. His future path now was to ignore law and write poetry with a view to eventually writing plays.

The Ambitious Stepmother, Rowe's first play, produced in 1700 at Lincoln's Inn Fields by Thomas Betterton and set in Persepolis, was well received.

This was followed in 1701 by Tamerlane. In this play the conqueror Timur represented William III, and Louis XIV is denounced as Bajazet. It was for many years regularly acted on the anniversary of William's landing at Torbay.

The Fair Penitent (1703), an adaptation of Massinger and Field's The Fatal Dowry, was pronounced by Dr Johnson as one of the most pleasing tragedies ever written in English. He noted that, "The story is domestic, and therefore easily received by the imagination, and assimilated to common life; the diction is exquisitely harmonious, and soft or spritely as occasion requires."

In 1704, he tried his hand at comedy, with The Biter at Lincoln's Inn Fields. The play is said to have amused no one except the author, and Rowe returned to tragedy in Ulysses (1706). For Johnson, this play was to share the fate of many such plays based on mythological heroes, as, "We have been too early acquainted with the poetical heroes to expect any pleasure from their revival"

The Royal Convert (1707) dealt with the persecutions endured by Aribert, son of Hengist and the Christian maiden Ethelinda. The story was set in England in an obscure and barbarous age. Rodogune was a tragic character, of high spirit and violent passions, yet with a wicked with a soul that would have been heroic if it had been virtuous.

Rowe is however well known for his work on Shakespeare's plays. He published the first 18th century edition of Shakespeare in six volumes in 1709. His practical knowledge of the stage helped him divide the plays into scenes and acts, with entrances and exits of the players noted. The spelling of names was normalized and each play prefixed with a dramatis personae. This 1709 edition was also the first to be illustrated, a frontispiece engraving being provided for each play. Unfortunately, Rowe based his text on the discredited Fourth Folio, a failing which many succeeding him also followed.

Rowe also wrote a short biography of William Shakespeare, entitled, Some Account of the Life of Mr. William Shakespear.

For two years (1709-11) he acted as under-secretary to the Duke of Queensberry when he was principal secretary of state for Scotland.

In Dublin in 1712 a revival of his earlier play, Tamerlane, at a time when political passions were running high, the performance provoked a serious riot.

The Tragedy of Jane Shore, played at Drury Lane with Mrs Oldfield in the title role in 1714. It ran for nineteen nights, and kept the stage longer than any other of Rowe's works. In the play, which consists chiefly of domestic scenes and private distress, the wife is forgiven because she repents, and the husband is honoured because he forgives.

The Tragedy of Lady Jane Grey followed in 1715, and as this play was not successful, it was his last foray into the medium.

Whilst his plays met with little success at the time his poems were received extremely well. Although he was not prolific nor his output large the quality was high.

With the accession to the throne of George I he was made a surveyor of customs, and then, in 1715, he succeeded Nahum Tate as poet laureate. It was the high point of his artistic life.

He was also appointed clerk of the council to the Prince of Wales, and in 1718 was nominated by Lord Chancellor Parker as clerk of the presentations in Chancery.

Nicholas Rowe died on December 6th, 1718, and was buried in Westminster Abbey.

Rowe married first a daughter of a Mr Parsons and left a son John. By his second wife Anne, née Devenish, he had a daughter Charlotte.

Index of Contents

ACT V
SCENE I
EPILOGUE (Spoken by Mrs. Bracegirdle, who played Lavinia)
Nicholas Rowe – A Concise Bibliography

To Her Grace the Duchess of Ormonde

MADAM,

The privilege of poetry (or it may be the vanity of the pretenders to it) has given 'em a kind of right to pretend, at the same time, to the favor of those whom their high birth and excellent qualities have placed in a very distinguishing manner above the rest of the world. If this be not a received maxim, yet I am sure I am to wish it were, that I may have at least some kind of excuse for laying this tragedy at your Grace's feet. I have too much reason to fear that it may prove but an indifferent entertainment to your Grace, since if I have any way succeeded in it, it has been in describing those violent passions which have been always strangers to so happy a temper and so noble and so exalted a virtue as your Grace is mistress of. Yet for all this I cannot but confess the vanity which I have, to hope that there may be some thing so moving in the misfortunes and distress of the play as may be not altogether unworthy of your Grace's pity. This is one of the main designs of tragedy, and to excite this generous pity in the greatest minds may pass for some kind of success in this way of writing. I am sensible of the presumption I am guilty of by this hope, and how much it is that I pretend to in your Grace's approbation; if it be my good fortune to meet with any little share of it, I shall always look upon it as much more to me than the general applause of the theater, or even the praise of a good critic. Your Grace's name is the best protection this play can hope for, since the world, ill-natured as it is, agrees in an universal respect and deference for your Grace's person and character.

In so censorious an age as this is, where malice furnishes out all the public conversations, where everybody pulls and is pulled to pieces of course, and where there is hardly such a thing as being merry but at another's expense, yet by a public and uncommon justice to the Duchess of Ormonde, her name has never been mentioned but as it ought, though she has beauty enough to provoke detraction from the fairest of her own sex, and virtue enough to make the loose and dissolute of the other (a very formidable party) her enemies. Instead of this, they agree to say nothing of her but what she deserves: that her spirit is worthy of her birth; her sweetness, of the love and respect of all the world; her piety, of her religion; her service, of her royal mistress; and her beauty and truth, of her lord; that in short every part of her character is just, and that she is the best reward for one of the greatest heroes this age has produced. This, madam, is what you must allow people everywhere to say; those whom you shall leave behind you in England will have something further to add: the loss we shall suffer by your Grace's journey to Ireland; the Queen's pleasure and the impatient wishes of that nation are about to deprive us of two of our public ornaments. But there is no arguing against reasons so prevalent as these. Those who shall lament your Grace's absence will yet acquiesce in the wisdom and justice of Her Majesty's choice, among all whose royal favors none could be so agreeable, upon a thousand accounts, to that people as the Duke of Ormonde. With what joy, what acclamations shall they meet a Governor who, beside their former obligations to his family, has so lately ventured his life and fortune for their preservation? What duty, what submission shall they not pay to that authority which the Queen has delegated to a person so dear to 'em? And with what honor, what respect shall they receive your Grace, when they look upon you as the noblest and best pattern Her Majesty could send 'em of her own royal goodness and personal virtues? They shall behold your Grace with the same pleasure the English shall

take whenever it shall be their good fortune to see you return to your native country. In England your Grace is become a public concern, and as your going away will be attended with a general sorrow, so your return shall give as general a joy; and to none of those many, more than to,
Madam,
Your Grace's most obedient, and most humble servant,
N. ROWE

*The Duchess of Ormonde was Mary, daughter of Henry Somerset, first Duke of Beaufort. She was the second wife of James Butler, second Duke of Ormonde. The Duke was appointed lord-lieutenant of Ireland in 1703, a position in which he served until 1707 and again from 1710 to 1712. After the death of Queen Anne he became a Jacobite.

DRAMATIS PERSONAE
MEN
SCIOLTO, a nobleman of Genoa, father to Calista
ALTAMONT, a young lord, in love with Calista, and designed her husband by Sciolto
HORATIO, his friend
LOTHARIO, a young lord, enemy to Altamont
ROSSANO, his friend
WOMEN
CALISTA, daughter to Sciolto
LAVINIA, sister to Altamont and wife to Horatio
LUCILLA, confidante to Calista
SERVANTS TO SCIOLTO

SCENE

Sciolto's palace and garden, with some part of the street near it, in Genoa.

THE FAIR PENITENT

PROLOGUE

Spoken by Mr Betterton

Long has the fate of kings and empires been
The common business of the tragic scene,
As if misfortune made the throne her seat,
And none could be unhappy but the great.
Dearly, 'tis true, each buys the crown he wears,
And many are the mighty monarch's cares;
By foreign foes and home-bred factions pressed,

Few are the joys he knows, and short his hours of rest.
Stories like these with wonder we may hear,
But far remote, and in a higher sphere,
We ne'er can pity what we ne'er can share:
Like distant battles of the Pole and Swede,
Which frugal citizens o'er coffee read,
Careless for who shall fail or who succeed.
Therefore an humbler theme our author chose,
A melancholy tale of private woes;
No princes here lost royalty bemoan,
But you shall meet with sorrows like your own;
Here see imperious love his vassals treat
As hardly as ambition does the great;
See how succeeding passions rage by turns,
How fierce the youth with joy and rapture burns,
And how to death, for beauty lost, he mourns.

Let no nice taste the poet's art arraign,
If some frail, vicious characters he feign;
Who writes should still let nature be his care,
Mix shades with lights, and not paint all things fair,
But show you men and women as they are.
With deference to the fair he bade me say,
Few to perfection ever found the way;
Many in many parts are known t'excel,
But 'twere too hard for one to act all well;
Whom justly life should through each scene commend,
The maid, the wife, the mistress, and the friend,
This age, 'tis true, has one great instance seen,
And heav'n in justice made that one a Queen.

ACT I

SCENE I - A Garden Belonging to Sciolto's Palace

Enter **ALTAMONT** and **HORATIO**.

ALTAMONT
Let this auspicious day be ever sacred,
No mourning, no misfortunes happen on it;
Let it be marked for triumphs and rejoicings;
Let happy lovers ever make it holy,
Choose it to bless their hopes and crown their wishes,
This happy day that gives me my Calista.

HORATIO

Yes, Altamont, today thy better stars
Are joined to shed their kindest influence on thee;
Sciolto's noble hand, that raised thee first,
Half dead and drooping o'er thy father's grave,
Completes its bounty and restores thy name
To that high rank and luster which it boasted
Before ungrateful Genoa had forgot
The merit of thy godlike father's arms;
Before that country which he long had served
In watchful councils and in winter camps
Had cast off his white age to want and wretchedness,
And made their court to faction by his ruin.

ALTAMONT
O great Sciolto! O my more than father!
Let me not live but at thy very name
My eager heart springs up and leaps with joy.
When I forget the vast, vast debt I owe thee,
Forget! (but 'tis impossible) then let me
Forget the use and privilege of reason,
Be driven from the commerce of mankind
To wander in the desert among brutes,
To bear the various fury of the seasons,
The night's unwholesome dew and noonday's heat,
To be the scorn of earth and curse of heav'n.

HORATIO
So open, so unbounded was his goodness,
It reached ev'n me, because I was thy friend.
When that great man I loved, thy noble father,
Bequeathed thy gentle sister to my arms,
His last dear pledge and legacy of friendship,
That happy tie made me Sciolto's son;
He called us his, and with a parent's fondness
Indulged us in his wealth, blessed us with plenty,
Healed all our cares, and sweetened love itself.

ALTAMONT
By heav'n, he found my fortunes so abandoned
That nothing but a miracle could raise 'em;
My father's bounty and the state's ingratitude
Had stripped him bare, nor left him ev'n a grave;
Undone myself, and sinking with his ruin,
I had no wealth to bring, nothing to succor him
But fruitless tears.

HORATIO
Yet what thou couldst thou didst,

And didst it like a son; when his hard creditors,
Urged and assisted by Lothario's father
(Foe to thy house and rival of their greatness),
By sentence of the cruel law, forbid
His venerable corpse to rest in earth,
Thou gav'st thyself a ransom for his bones;
With piety uncommon didst give up
Thy hopeful youth to slaves who ne'er knew mercy,
Sour, unrelenting, money-loving villains
Who laugh at human nature and forgiveness,
And are like fiends, the factors for destruction.
Heav'n, who beheld the pious act, approved it,
And bade Sciolto's bounty be its proxy,
To bless thy filial virtue with abundance.

ALTAMONT
But see he comes, the author of my happiness,
The man who saved my life from deadly sorrow,
Who bids my days be blessed with peace and plenty,
And satisfies my soul with love and beauty.

[Enter **SCIOLTO**; he runs to **ALTAMONT** and embraces him.

SCIOLTO
Joy to thee, Altamont! Joy to myself!
Joy to this happy morn that makes thee mine,
That kindly grants what nature had denied me,
And makes me father of a son like thee.

ALTAMONT
My father! O, let me unlade my breast,
Pour out the fullness of my soul before you,
Show ev'ry tender, ev'ry grateful thought
This wond'rous goodness stirs. But 'tis impossible,
And utterance all is vile, since I can only
Swear you reign here, but never tell how much.
It is enough; I know thee—thou art honest;
Goodness innate and worth hereditary
Are in thy mind; thy noble father's virtues
Spring freshly forth and blossom in thy youth.

ALTAMONT
Thus heav'n from nothing raised his fair creation,
And then with wond'rous joy beheld its beauty,
Well pleased to see the excellence he gave.

SCIOLTO
O noble youth! I swear since first I knew thee,

Ev'n from that day of sorrows when I saw thee,
Adorned and lovely in thy filial tears,
The mourner and redeemer of thy father,
I set thee down and sealed thee for my own;
Thou art my son, ev'n near me as Calista.
Horatio and Lavinia too are mine;

[Embraces **HORATIO**.

All are my children, and shall share my heart.
But wherefore waste we thus this happy day?
The laughing minutes summon thee to joy,
And with new pleasures court thee as they pass;
Thy waiting bride ev'n chides thee for delaying,
And swears thou com'st not with a bridegroom's haste.

ALTAMONT
O, could I hope there was one thought of Altamont,
One kind remembrance in Calista's breast,
The winds, with all their wings, would be too slow
To bear me to her feet. For, O, my father,
Amidst this stream of joy that bears me on,
Blessed as I am and honored in your friendship,
There is one pain that hangs upon my heart.

SCIOLTO
What means my son?

ALTAMONT
When, at your intercession,
Last night Calista yielded to my happiness,
Just ere we parted, as I sealed my vows
With rapture on her lips, I found her cold,
As a dead lover's statue on his tomb;
A rising storm of passion shook her breast,
Her eyes a piteous show'r of tears let fall,
And then she sighed as if her heart were breaking.
With all the tend'rest eloquence of love
I begged to be a sharer in her grief;
But she, with looks averse and eyes that froze me,
Sadly replied, her sorrows were her own,
Nor in a father's pow'r to dispose of.

SCIOLTO
Away! It is the cozenage of their sex,
One of the common arts they practice on us,
To sigh and weep then when their hearts beat high
With expectation of the coming joy;

Thou hast in camps and fighting fields been bred,
Unknowing in the subtleties of women;
The virgin bride who swoons with deadly fear
To see the end of all her wishes near,
When, blushing, from the light and public eyes
To the kind covert of the night she flies,
With equal fires to meet the bridegroom moves,
Melts in his arms, and with a loose she loves.

[Exeunt.

[Enter **LOTHARIO** and **ROSSANO**.

LOTHARIO
The father and the husband!

ROSSANO
Let them pass,
They saw us not.

LOTHARIO
I care not if they did;
Ere long I mean to meet 'em face to face
And gall 'em with my triumph o'er Calista.

ROSSANO
You loved her once.

LOTHARIO
I liked her, would have married her,
But that it pleased her father to refuse me,
To make this honorable fool her husband.
For which, if I forget him, may the shame
I mean to brand his name with, stick on mine.

ROSSANO
She, gentle soul, was kinder than her father.

LOTHARIO
She was, and oft in private gave me hearing,
Till, by long list'ning to the soothing tale,
At length her easy heart was wholly mine.

ROSSANO
I have heard you oft describe her, haughty, insolent,
And fierce with high disdain; it moves my wonder
That virtue thus defended should be yielded
A pray to loose desires.

LOTHARIO
Hear, then, I'll tell thee.
Once in a lone and secret hour of night,
When ev'ry eye was closed, and the pale moon
And stars alone shone conscious of the theft,
Hot with the Tuscan grape and high in blood,
Hap'ly I stole unheeded to her chamber.

ROSSANO
That minute sure was lucky.

LOTHARIO
O 'twas great.
I found the fond, believing, love-sick maid
Loose, unattired, warm, tender, full of wishes;
Fierceness and pride, the guardians of her honor,
Were charmed to rest, and love alone was waking.
Within her rising bosom all was calm
As peaceful seas that know no storms and only
Are gently lifted up and down by tides.
I snatched the glorious, golden opportunity,
And with prevailing, youthful ardor pressed her,
Till with short sighs and murmuring reluctance
The yielding fair one gave me perfect happiness.
Ev'n all the livelong night we passed in bliss,
In ecstasies too fierce to last forever;
At length the morn and cold indifference came;
When fully sated with the luscious banquet,
I hastily took leave and left the nymph
To think on what was past, and sigh alone.

ROSSANO
You saw her soon again.

LOTHARIO
Too soon I saw her;
For, O, that meeting was not like the former;
I found my heart no more beat high with transport,
No more I sighed and languished for enjoyment;
'Twas past, and reason took her turn to reign,
While ev'ry weakness fell before her throne.

ROSSANO
What of the lady?

LOTHARIO
With uneasy fondness

She hung upon me, wept, and sighed, and swore
She was undone, talked of a priest and marriage,
Of flying with me from her father's pow'r,
Called ev'ry saint and blessed angel down
To witness for her that she was my wife.
I started at that name.

ROSSANO
What answer made you?

LOTHARIO
None; but pretending sudden pain and illness,
Escaped the persecution; two nights since,
By message urged, and frequent importunity,
Again I saw her. Straight with tears and sighs,
With swelling breasts, with swooning, with distraction,
With all the subtleties and pow'rful arts
Of willful woman lab'ring for her purpose,
Again she told the same dull, nauseous tale.
Unmoved, I begged her spare th'ungrateful subject,
Since I resolved, that love and peace of mind
Might flourish long inviolate betwixt us,
Never to load it with the marriage chain;
That I would still retain her in my heart,
My ever gentle mistress and my friend;
But for those other names of wife and husband,
They only meant ill nature, cares, and quarrels.

ROSSANO
How bore she this reply?

LOTHARIO
Ev'n as the earth
When (winds pent up or eating fires beneath,
Shaking the mass) she labors with destruction.
At first her rage was dumb and wanted words,
But when the storm found way, 'twas wild and loud.
Mad as the priestess of the Delphic god,
Enthusiastic passion swelled her breast,
Enlarged her voice, and ruffled all her form;
Proud, and disdainful of the love I proffered,
She called me "Villain! Monster! Base betrayer!"
At last, in very bitterness of soul,
With deadly imprecations on herself,
She vowed severely ne'er to see me more,
Then bid me fly that minute; I obeyed,
And, bowing, left her to grow cool at leisure.

ROSSANO
She has relented since, else why this message
To meet the keeper of her secrets here This morning?

LOTHARIO
See the person whom you named.

[Enter **LUCILLA**.

Well, my ambassadress, what must we treat of?
Come you to menace war and proud defiance,
Or does the peaceful olive grace your message?
Is your fair mistress calmer? Does she soften?
And must we love again? Perhaps she means
To treat in juncture with her new ally,
And make her husband party to th' agreement.

LUCILLA
Is this well done, my lord? Have you put off
All sense of human nature? Keep a little,
A little pity to distinguish manhood,
Lest other men, though cruel, should disclaim you,
And judge you to be numbered with the brutes.

LOTHARIO
I see thou'st learned to rail.

LUCILLA
I've learned to weep;
That lesson my sad mistress often gives me;
By day she seeks some melancholy shade
To hide her sorrows from the prying world;
At night she watches all the long, long hours,
And listens to the winds and beating rain,
With sighs as loud and tears that fall as fast.
Then ever and anon she wrings her hands,
And cries, "False, false Lothario!"

LOTHARIO
O, no more!
I swear thou'lt spoil thy pretty face with crying,
And thou hast beauty that may make thy fortune;
Some keeping cardinal shall dote upon thee,
And barter his church treasure for thy freshness.

LUCILLA
What! Shall I sell my innocence and youth
For wealth or titles to perfidious man!

To man, who makes his mirth of our undoing!
The base, professed betrayer of our sex!
Let me grow old in all misfortunes else,
Rather than know the sorrows of Galista.

LOTHARIO
Does she send thee to chide in her behalf?
I swear thou dost it with so good a grace
That I could almost love thee for thy frowning.

LUCILLA
Read there, my lord, there, in her own sad lines,

[Giving a letter.

Which best can tell the story of her woes,
That grief of heart which your unkindness gives her.

LOTHARIO [reads]
"Your cruelty—obedience to my father—give my hand to Altamont."
[Aside] By heav'n, 'tis well; such ever be the gifts
With which I greet the man whom my soul hates.
But to go on!
"—Wish—heart—honor—too faithless—weakness—to-morrow—last trouble—lost Calista."
Women, I see, can change as well as men;
She writes me here, forsaken as I am,
That I should bind my brows with mournful willow,
For she has given her hand to Altamont.
Yet tell the fair inconstant—

LUCILLA
How, my lord?

LOTHARIO
Nay, no more angry words; say to Calista,
The humblest of her slaves shall wait her pleasure,
If she can leave her happy husband's arms
To think upon so lost a thing as I am.

LUCILLA
Alas! For pity come with gentler looks;
Wound not her heart with this unmanly triumph;
And though you love her not, yet swear you do,
So shall dissembling once be virtuous in you.

LOTHARIO
Ha! Who comes here?

LUCILLA
The bridegroom's friend, Horatio.
He must not see us here; tomorrow early
Be at the garden gate.

LOTHARIO
Bear to my love
My kindest thought, and swear I will not fail her.
Lothario, putting up the letter hastily, drops it as he goes out.

[Exeunt **LOTHARIO** and **ROSSANO** one way, **LUCILLA** another.

[Enter **HORATIO**.

HORATIO
Sure 'tis the very error of my eyes:
Waking I dream, or I beheld Lothario;
He seemed conferring with Calista's woman;
At my approach they started, and retired.
What business could he have here, and with her?
I know he bears the noble Altamont
Professed and deadly hate— What paper's this?

[Taking up the letter.

Ha! To Lothario—'sdeath! Calista's name!

[Opening it.

Confusion and misfortune!

[Reads.

"Your cruelty has at length determined me, and I have resolved this morning to yield a perfect obedience to my father and to give my hand to Altamont, in spite of my weakness for the false Lothario. I could almost wish I had that heart and that honor to bestow with it which you have robbed me of—"
Damnation! To the test—

[Reads again.

"But, O, I fear, could I retrieve 'em I should again be undone by the too faithless, yet too lovely Lothario; this is the last weakness of my pen, and tomorrow shall be the last in which I will indulge my eyes. Lucilla shall conduct you, if you are kind enough to let me see you; it shall be the last trouble you shall meet with from
The lost Calista."

The lost indeed! For thou art gone as far
As there can be perdition. Fire and sulphur,

Hell is the sole avenger of such crimes.
O that the ruin were but all thy own!
Thou wilt ev'n make thy father curse his age;
At sight of this black scroll the gentle Altamont
(For, O, I know his heart is set upon thee)
Shall droop and hang his discontented head,
Like merit scorned by insolent authority,
And never grace the public with his virtues.—
Perhaps ev'n now he gazes fondly on her,
And, thinking soul and body both alike,
Blesses the perfect workmanship of heav'n;
Then sighing, to his ev'ry care speaks peace,
And bids his heart be satisfied with happiness.
O wretched husband! While she hangs about thee
With idle blandishments and plays the fond one,
Ev'n then her hot imagination wanders,
Contriving riot and loose scapes of love;
And while she claps thee close, makes thee a monster.
What if I give this paper to her father?
It follows that his justice dooms her dead,
And breaks his heart with sorrow; hard return
For all the good his hand has heaped on us.
Hold, let me take a moment's thought.

[Enter **LAVINIA**.

LAVINIA
My lord!
Trust me, it joys my heart that I have found you.
Enquiring wherefore you had left the company
Before my brother's nuptial rites were ended,
They told me you had felt some sudden illness.
Where are you sick? Is it your head? your heart?
Tell me, my love, and ease my anxious thoughts,
That I may take you gently in my arms,
Soothe you to rest, and soften all your pains.

HORATIO
It were unjust; no, let me spare my friend,
Lock up the fatal secret in my breast,
Nor tell him that which will undo his quiet.

LAVINIA
What means my lord?

HORATIO
Ha! Saidst thou, my Lavinia?

LAVINIA

Alas, you know not what you make me suffer.
Why are you pale? Why did you start and tremble?
Whence is that sigh? And wherefore are your eyes
Severely raised to heav'n? The sick man thus,
Acknowledging the summons of his fate,
Lifts up his feeble hands and eyes for mercy,
And with confusion thinks upon his audit.

HORATIO

O, no! Thou hast mistook my sickness quite;
These pangs are of the soul. Would I had met
Sharpest convulsions, spotted pestilences,
Or any other deadly foe to life,
Rather than heave beneath this load of thought.

LAVINIA

Alas, what is it? Wherefore turn you from me?
Why did you falsely call me your Lavinia,
And swear I was Horatio's better half,
Since now you mourn unkindly by yourself,
And rob me of my partnership of sadness?
Witness, you holy pow'rs, who know my truth,
There cannot be a chance in life so miserable,
Nothing so very hard but I could bear it
Much rather than my love should treat me coldly,
And use me like a stranger to his heart.

HORATIO

Seek not to know what I would hide from all,
But most from thee. I never knew a pleasure,
Aught that was joyful, fortunate, or good,
But straight I ran to bless thee with the tidings,
And laid up all my happiness with thee;
But wherefore, wherefore should I give thee pain?
Then spare me, I conjure thee, ask no further;
Allow my melancholy thoughts this privilege,
And let 'em brood in secret o'er their sorrows.

LAVINIA

It is enough; chide not, and all is well;
Forgive me if I saw you sad, Horatio,
And asked to weep out part of your misfortunes;
I wo' not press to know what you forbid me.
Yet, my loved lord, yet you must grant me this:
Forget your cares for this one happy day,
Devote this day to mirth and to your Altamont;
For his dear sake let peace be in your looks.

Ev'n now the jocund bridegroom wants your wishes;
He thinks the priest has but half blessed his marriage
Till his friend hails him with the sound of joy.

HORATIO

O, never, never, never! Thou art innocent;
Simplicity from ill, pure native truth,
And candor of the mind adorn thee ever;
But there are such, such false ones in the world,
'Twould fill they gentle soul with wild amazement
To hear their story told.

LAVINIA

False ones, my lord?

HORATIO

Fatally fair they are, and in their smiles
The graces, little loves, and young desires inhabit;
But all that gaze upon 'em are undone,
For they are false, luxurious in their appetites,
And all the heav'n they hope for is variety;
One lover to another still succeeds,
Another, and another after that,
And the last fool is welcome as the former,
Till, having loved his hour out, he gives place,
And mingles with the herd that went before him.

LAVINIA

Can there be such? And have they peace of mind?
Have they in all the series of their changing
One happy hour? If women are such things,
How was I formed so different from my sex?
My little heart is satisfied with you;
You take up all her room, as in a cottage
Which harbors some benighted princely stranger,
Where the good man, pround of his hospitality,
Yields all his homely dwelling to his guest,
And hardly keeps a corner to himself.

HORATIO

O, were they all like thee, men would adore 'em,
And all the business of their lives be loving;
The nuptial band should be the pledge of peace,
And all domestic cares and quarrels cease;
The world should learn to love by virtuous rules,
And marriage be no more the jest of fools.

SCENE I – A Hall

Enter **CALISTA** and **LUCILLA**.

CALISTA
Be dumb forever, silent as the grave,
Nor let thy fond, officious love disturb
My solemn sadness with the sound of joy.
If thou wilt soothe me, tell some dismal tale
Of pining discontent and black despair;
For, O, I've gone around through all my thoughts,
But all are indignation, love, or shame,
And my dear peace of mind is lost forever.

LUCILLA
Why do you follow still that wand'ring fire
That has misled your weary steps and leaves you
Benighted in a wilderness of woe?
That false Lothario! Turn from the deceiver;
Turn, and behold where gentle Altamont,
Kind as the softest virgin of our sex,
And faithful as the simple village swain
That never knew the courtly vice of changing,
Sighs at your feet and woos you to be happy.

CALISTA
Away—I think not of him. My sad soul
Has formed a dismal, melancholy scene,
Such a retreat as I would wish to find;
An unfrequented vale, o'ergrown with trees
Mossy and old, within whose lonesome shade
Ravens and birds ill-omened only dwell;
No sound to break the silence but a brook
That, bubbling, winds among the weeds; no mark
Of any human shape that had been there,
Unless a skeleton of some poor wretch
Who had long since, like me, by love undone,
Sought that sad place out to despair and die in.

LUCILLA
Alas for pity!

CALISTA
There I fain would hide me
From the base world, from malice, and from shame;
For 'tis the solemn counsel of my soul

Never to live with public loss of honor;
'Tis fixed to die, rather than bear the insolence
Of each affected she that tells my story,
And blesses her good stars that she is virtuous.
To be a tale for fools! Scorned by the women,
And pitied by the men! O, insupportable!

LUCILLA

Can you perceive the manifest destruction,
The gaping gulf that opens just before you,
And yet rush on, though conscious of the danger?
O, hear me, hear your ever faithful creature;
By all the good I wish, by all the ill
My trembling heart forebodes, let me entreat you
Never to see this faithless man again;
Let me forbid his coming.

CALISTA

On thy life
I charge thee, no; my genius drives me on;
I must, I will behold him once again;
Perhaps it is the crisis of my fate,
And this one interview shall end my cares.
My lab'ring heart, that swells with indignation,
Heaves to discharge the burden; that once done,
The busy thing shall rest within its cell,
And never beat again.

LUCILLA

Trust not to that;
Rage is the shortest passion of our souls;
Like narrow brooks that rise with sudden show'rs,
It swells in haste, and falls again as soon;
Still as it ebbs, the softer thoughts flow in,
And the deceiver, love, supplies its place.

CALISTA

I have been wronged enough to arm my temper
Against the smooth delusion; but alas!
(Chide not my weakness, gentle maid, but pity me),
A woman's softness hangs about me still;
Then let me blush, and tell thee all my folly.
I swear I could not see the dear betrayer
Kneel at my feet and sigh to be forgiven,
But my relenting heart would pardon all,
And quite forget 'twas he that had undone me.

LUCILLA

Ye sacred powers, whose gracious providence
Is watchful for our good, guard me from men,
From their deceitful tongues, their vows and flatteries;
Still let me pass neglected by their eyes,
Let my bloom wither and my form decay,
That none may think it worth his while to ruin me,
And fatal love may never be my bane.

CALISTA
Ha! Altamont? Calista, now be wary,
And guard thy soul's accesses with dissembling;
Nor let this hostile husband's eyes explore
The warring passions and tumultuous thoughts
That rage within thee and deform thy reason.

[Enter **ALTAMONT**.

ALTAMONT
Be gone, my cares, I give you to the winds,
Far to be borne, far from the happy Altamont;
For from this sacred era of my love
A better order of succeeding days
Come smiling forward, white and lucky all.
Calista is the mistress of the year;
She crowns the seasons with auspicious beauty,
And bids ev'n all my hours be good and joyful.

CALISTA
If I was ever mistress of such happiness,
O, wherefore did I play th'unthrifty fool,
And, wasting all on others, leave myself
Without one thought of joy to give me comfort?

ALTAMONT
O mighty Love! Shall that fair face profane
This thy great festival with frowns and sadness!
I swear it sha' not be, for I will woo thee
With sighs so moving, with so warm a transport
That thou shalt catch the gentle flame from me,
And kindle into joy.

CALISTA
I tell thee, Altamont,
Such hearts as ours were never paired above;
Ill suited to each other; joined, not matched;
Some sullen influence, a foe to both,
Has wrought this fatal marriage to undo us.
Mark but the frame and temper of our minds,

How very much we differ. Ev'n this day,
That fills thee with such ecstasy and transport,
To me brings nothing that should make me bless it,
Or think it better than the day before,
Or any other in the course of time
That dully took its turn and was forgotten.

ALTAMONT
If to behold thee as my pledge of happiness,
To know none fair, none excellent beside thee,
If still to love thee with unwearied constancy,
Through ev'ry season, ev'ry change of life,
Through wrinkled age, through sickness and misfortune,
Be worth the least return of grateful love,
O, then let my Calista bless this day,
And set it down for happy.

CALISTA
'Tis the day
In which my father gave my hand to Altamont;
As such I will remember it forever.

[Enter **SCIOLTO**, **HORATIO** and **LAVINIA**.

SCIOLTO.
Let mirth go on, let pleasure know no pause,
But fill up ev'ry minute of this day.
'Tis yours, my children, sacred to your loves;
The glorious sun himself for you looks gay;
He shines for Altamont and for Calista.
Let there be music; let the master touch
The sprightly string and softly breathing flute
Till harmony rouse ev'ry gentle passion,
Teach the cold maid to lose her fears in love,
And the fierce youth to languish at her feet.
Begin. Ev'n age itself is cheered with music;
It wakes a glad remembrance of our youth,
Calls back past joys, and warms us into transport.
Here an entertainment of music and dancing.

SONG
By Mr. Congreve

I
Ah, stay! Ah, turn! Ah, whither would you fly,
Too charming, too relentless maid?
I follow not to conquer but to die;
You of the fearful are afraid.

II

In vain I call; for she, like fleeting air
When pressed by some tempestuous wind,
Flies swifter from the voice of my despair,
Nor casts one pitying look behind.

SCIOLTO

Take care my gates are open, bid all welcome;
All who rejoice with me today are friends;
Let each indulge his genius, each be glad,
Jocund, and free, and swell the feast with mirth.
The sprightly bowl shall cheerfully go round,
None shall be grave, nor too severely wise;
Losses and disappointments, cares and poverty,
The rich man's insolence and great man's scorn,
In wine shall be forgotten all. Tomorrow
Will be too soon to think, and to be wretched.
O, grant, ye powers, that I may see these happy,

[Pointing to **ALTAMONT** and **CALISTA**.

Completely blest, and I have life enough;
And leave the rest indifferently to fate.

[Exeunt. Manet **HORATIO**.

HORATIO

What if, while all are here intent on reveling,
I privately went forth and sought Lothario?
This letter may be forged; perhaps the wantonness
Of his vain youth, to stain a lady's fame;
Perhaps his malice, to disturb my friend.
O, no! My heart forebodes it must be true.
Methought ev'n now I marked the starts of guilt
That shook her soul, though damned dissimulation
Screened her dark thoughts, and set to public view
A specious face of innocence and beauty.
O, false appearance! What is all our sovereignty,
Our boasted pow'r? When they oppose their arts,
Still they prevail, and we are found their fools.
With such smooth looks and many a gentle word
The first fair she beguiled her easy lord;
Too blind with love and beauty to beware,
He fell unthinking in the fatal snare;
Nor could believe that such a heav'nly face
Had bargained with the devil to damn her wretched race.

[Exit.

Enter **LOTHARIO** and **ROSSANO**.

LOTHARIO
To tell thee, then, the purport of my thoughts,
The loss of this fond paper would not give me
A moment of disquiet were it not
My instrument of vengeance on this Altamont;
Therefore I mean to wait some opportunity
Of speaking with the maid we saw this morning.

ROSSANO
I wish you, sir, to think upon the danger
Of being seen; today their friends are round 'em,
And any eye that lights by chance on you
Shall put your life and safety to the hazard.

[They confer aside.

[Enter **HORATIO**.

HORATIO
Still I must doubt some mystery of mischief,
Some artifice beneath; Lothario's father—
I knew him well; he was sagacious, cunning,
Fluent in words, and bold in peaceful councils,
But of a cold, unactive hand in war.
Yet with these coward's virtues he undid
My unsuspecting, valiant, honest friend.
This son, if fame mistakes not, is more hot,
More open, and unartful. Ha! He's here!Seeing him.

LOTHARIO
Damnation! He again! This second time
Today he has crossed me like my evil genius.

HORATIO
I sought you, sir.

LOTHARIO
'Tis well then I am found.

HORATIO

'Tis well you are. The man who wrongs my friend
To the earth's utmost verge I would pursue;
No place, though e'er so holy, should protect him;
No shape that artful fear e'er formed should hide him,
Till he fair answer made, and did me justice.

LOTHARIO

Ha! Dost thou know me, that I am Lothario?
As great a name as this proud city boasts of.
Who is this mighty man, then, this Horatio,
That I should basely hide me from his anger,
Lest he should chide me for his friend's displeasure?

HORATIO

The brave, 'tis true, do never shun the light;
Just are their thoughts, and open are their tempers,
Freely without disguise they love and hate,
Still are they found in the fair face of day,
And heav'n and men are judges of their actions.

LOTHARIO

Such let 'em be of mine; there's not a purpose
Which my soul ever framed or my hand acted,
But I could well have bid the world look on,
And what I once durst do, have dared to justify.

HORATIO

Where was this open boldness, this free spirit,
When but this very morning I surprised thee
In base, dishonest privacy, consulting
And bribing a poor, mercenary wretch
To sell her lady's secrets, stain her honor,
And with a forged contrivance blast her virtue?
At sight of me thou fled'st!

LOTHARIO

Ha! Fled from thee?

HORATIO

Thou fled'st, and guilt was on thee; like a thief,
A pilferer descried in some dark corner,
Who there had lodged with mischievous intent
To rob and ravage at the hour of rest,
And do a midnight murder on the sleepers.

LOTHARIO

Slave! Villain!

[Offers to draw: **ROSSANO** holds him.

ROSSANO
Hold, my lord! Think where you are,
Think how unsafe and hurtful to your honor
It were to urge a quarrel in this place,
And shock the peaceful city with a broil.

LOTHARIO
Then since thou dost provoke my vengeance, know
I would not for this city's worth, for all
Which the sea wafts to our Ligurian shore,
But that the joys I reaped with that fond wanton,
The wife of Altamont, should be as public
As is the noonday sun, air, earth, or water,
Or any common benefit of nature.
Think'st thou I meant the shame should be concealed?
O, no! By hell and vengeance, all I wanted
Was some fit messenger to bear the news
To the dull, doting husband; now I have found him,
And thou art he.

HORATIO
I hold thee base enough
To break through law, and spurn at sacred order,
And do a brutal injury like this;
Yet mark me well, young lord, I think Calista
Too nice, too noble, and too great of soul
To be the prey of such a thing as thou art.
'Twas base and poor, unworthy of a man,
To forge a scroll so villainous and loose,
And mark it with a noble lady's name;
These are the mean, dishonest arts of cowards,
Strangers to manhood and to glorious dangers,
Who, bred at home in idleness and riot,
Ransack for mistresses th'unwholesome stews,
And never know the worth of virtuous love.

LOTHARIO
Think'st thou I forged the letter? Think so still,
Till the broad shame comes staring in thy face,
And boys shall hoot the cuckold as he passes.

HORATIO
Away—no woman could descend so low;
A skipping, dancing, worthless tribe you are;
Fit only for yourselves, you herd together;
And when the circling glass warms your vain hearts,

You talk of beauties that you never saw
And fancy raptures that you never knew.
Legends of saints who never yet had being,
Or, being, ne'er were saints, are not so false
As the fond tales which you recount of love.

LOTHARIO
But that I do not hold it worth my leisure,
I could produce such damning proof—

HORATIO
'Tis false!
You blast the fair with lies because they scorn you,
Plate you like age, like ugliness and impotence;
Rather than make you blest, they would die virgins,
And stop the propagation of mankind.

LOTHARIO
It is the curse of fools to be secure,
And that be thine and Altamont's. Dream on,
Nor think upon my vengeance till thou feel'st it.

HORATIO
Flold, sir, another word, and then farewell.
Though I think greatly of Calista's virtue,
And hold it far beyond thy pow'r to hurt,
Yet as she shares the honor of my Altamont,
That treasure of a soldier, bought with blood,
And kept at life's expense, I must not have
(Mark me, young sir) her very name profaned.
Learn to restrain the license of your speech;
'Tis held you are too lavish. When you are met
Among your set of fools, talk of your dress,
Of dice, of whores, of horses, and yourselves;
'Tis safer, and becomes your understandings.

LOTHARIO
What if we pass beyond this solemn order,
And, in defiance of the stern Horatio,
Indulge our gayer thoughts, let laughter loose,
And use his sacred friendship for our mirth?

HORATIO
'Tis well! Sir, you are pleasant—

LOTHARIO
By the joys
Which yet my soul has uncontrolled pursued,

I would not turn aside from my least pleasure
Though all thy force were armed to bar my way;
But like the birds, great Nature's happy commoners,
That haunt in woods, in meads, in flow'ry gardens,
Rifle the sweets, and taste her choicest fruits,
Yet scorn to ask the lordly owners leave.

HORATIO
What liberty has vain, presumptuous youth,
That thou shouldst dare provoke me unchastised?
But henceforth, boy, I warn thee, shun my walks;
If in the bounds of yon forbidden place
Again thou'rt found, expect a punishment
Such as great souls, impatient of an injury,
Exact from those who wrong 'em much, ev'n death,
Or something worse; an injured husband's vengeance
Shall print a thousand wounds, tear thy fine form,
And scatter thee to all the winds of heav'n.

LOTHARIO
Is then my way in Genoa prescribed
By a dependent on the wretched Altamont,
A talking sir that brawls for him in taverns,
And vouches for his valor's reputation?

HORATIO
Away—thy speech is fouler than thy manners.

LOTHARIO
Or if there be a name more vile, his parasite,
A beggar's parasite!

HORATIO
Now learn humanity,

[Offers to strike him; **ROSSANO** interposes.

Since brutes and boys are only taught with blows.

LOTHARIO
Damnation!

[They draw.

ROSSANO
Hold, this goes no further here.
Horatio, 'tis too much; already see
The crowd are gath'ring to us.

LOTHARIO
O, Rossano!
Or give me way, or thou'rt no more my friend.

ROSSANO
Sciolto's servants too have ta'en the alarm;
You'll be oppressed by numbers; be advised,
Or I must force you hence; take't on my word,
You shall have justice done you on Horatio.
Put up, my lord.

LOTHARIO
This wo' not brook delay;
West of the town a mile, among the rocks,
Two hours ere noon tomorrow I expect thee,
Thy single hand to mine.

HORATIO
I'll meet thee there.

LOTHARIO
Tomorrow, O my better stars! Tomorrow
Exert your influence, shine strongly for me;
'Tis not a common conquest I would gain,
Since love, as well as arms, must grace my triumph.

[Exeunt **LOTHARIO** and **ROSSANO**.

HORATIO
Two hours ere noon tomorrow! Ha! Ere that
He sees Calista! O unthinking fool—
What if I urged her with the crime and danger?
If any spark from heav'n remain unquenched
Within her breast, my breath perhaps may wake it;
Could I but prosper there, I would not doubt
My combat with that loud, vainglorious boaster.
Were you, ye fair, but cautious whom ye trust,
Did you but think how seldom fools are just,
So many of your sex would not in vain
Of broken vows and faithless men complain.
Of all the various wretches love has made,
How few have been by men of sense betrayed?
Convinced by reason, they your pow'r confess,
Pleased to be happy, as you're pleased to bless,
And conscious of your worth, can never love you less.

[Exit.

Enter **SCIOLTO** and **CALISTA**.

SCIOLTO
Now by my life, my honor, 'tis too much.
Have I not marked thee wayward as thou art,
Perverse and sullen all this day of joy?
When ev'ry heart was cheered, and mirth went round,
Sorrow, displeasure, and repining anguish
Sat on thy brow, like some malignant planet,
Foe to the harvest and the healthy year,
Who scowls adverse, and lowers upon the world,
When all the other stars, with gentle aspect,
Propitious shine, and meaning good to man.

CALISTA
Is then the task of duty half performed?
Has not your daughter giv'n herself to Altamont,
Yielded the native freedom of her will
To an imperious husband's lordly rule
To gratify a father's stern command?

SCIOLTO
Dost thou complain?

CALISTA
For pity, do not frown then,
If in despite of all my vowed obedience,
A sigh breaks out, or a tear falls by chance;
For, O, that sorrow which has drawn your anger
Is the sad native of Calista's breast,
And, once possessed, will never quit its dwelling
Till life, the prop of all, shall leave the building
To tumble down and moulder into ruin.

SCIOLTO
Now by the sacred dust of that dear saint
That was thy mother, by her wond'rous goodness,
Her soft, her tender, most complying sweetness,
I swear some sullen thought that shuns the light
Lurks underneath that sadness in thy visage.
But mark me well: though by yon heav'n I love thee

As much, I think, as a fond parent can,
Yet shouldst thou (which the pow'rs above forbid)
E'er stain the honor of thy name with infamy,
I cast thee off as one whose impious hands
Had rent asunder nature's nearest ties,
Which, once divided, never join again.
Today I have made a noble youth thy husband;
Consider well his worth, reward his love,
Be willing to be happy, and thou art so.

[Exit **SCIOLTO**.

CALISTA
How hard is the condition of our sex,
Through ev'ry state of life the slaves of man!
In all the dear, delightful days of youth
A rigid father dictates to our wills,
And deals out pleasure with a scanty hand;
To his, the tyrant husband's reign succeeds;
Proud with opinion of superior reason,
He holds domestic business and devotion
All we are capable to know, and shuts us,
Like cloistered idiots, from the world's acquaintance
And all the joys of freedom; wherefore are we
Born with high souls but to assert ourselves,
Shake off this vile obedience they exact,
And claim an equal empire o'er the world?

[Enter **HORATIO**.

HORATIO
She's here! Yet, O, my tongue is at a loss;
Teach me, some pow'r, that happy art of speech
To dress my purpose up in gracious words,
Such as may softly steal upon her soul
And never waken the tempestuous passions.
By heav'n, she weeps!—Forgive me, fair Calista,
If I presume, on privilege of friendship,
To join my grief to yours, and mourn the evils
That hurt your peace and quench those eyes in tears.

CALISTA
To steal unlooked-for on my private sorrow
Speaks not the man of honor nor the friend,
But rather means the spy.

HORATIO
Unkindly said!

For, O, as sure as you accuse me falsely,
I come to prove myself Calista's friend.

CALISTA
You are my husband's friend, the friend of Altamont.

HORATIO
Are you not one? Are you not joined by heav'n,
Each interwoven with the other's fate?
Are you not mixed like streams of meeting rivers
Whose blended waters are no more distinguished,
But roll into the sea, one common flood?
Then who can give his friendship but to one?
Who can be Altamont's, and not Calista's?

CALISTA
Force, and the wills of our imperious rulers
May bind two bodies in one wretched chain;
But minds will still look back to their own choice.
So the poor captive in a foreign realm
Stands on the shore, and sends his wishes back
To the dear native land from whence he came.

HORATIO
When souls that should agree to will the same,
To have one common object for their wishes,
Look different ways, regardless of each other,
Think what a train of wretchedness ensues:
Love shall be banished from the genial bed,
The nights shall all be lonely and unquiet,
And ev'ry day shall be a day of cares.

CALISTA
Then all the boasted office of thy friendship
Was but to tell Calista what a wretch she is.
Alas, what needed that?

HORATIO
O, rather say
I came to tell her how she might be happy;
To soothe the secret anguish of her soul,
To comfort that fair mourner, that forlorn one,
And teach her steps to know the paths of peace.

CALISTA
Say thou to whom this paradise is known,
Where lies the blissful region?
Mark my way to it,

For, O, 'tis sure, I long to be at rest.

HORATIO
Then—to be good is to be happy. Angels
Are happier than mankind, because they are better.
Guilt is the source of sorrow; 'tis the fiend,
The avenging fiend, that follows us behind
With whips and stings; the blest know none of this,
But rest in everlasting peace of mind,
And find the height of all their heav'n is goodness.

CALISTA
And what bold parasite's officious tongue
Shall dare to tax Calista's name with guilt?

HORATIO
None should; but 'tis a busy, talking world,
That with licentious breath blows like the wind,
As freely on the palace as the cottage.

CALISTA
What mystic riddle lurks beneath thy words,
Which thou wouldst seem unwilling to express,
As if it meant dishonor to my virtue?
Away with this ambiguous, shuffling phrase,
And let thy oracle be understood.

HORATIO
Lothario!

CALISTA
Fla! What wouldst thou mean by him?

HORATIO
Lothario and Calista! Thus they join
Two names which heav'n decreed should never meet
Hence have the talkers of this populous city
A shameful tale to tell for public sport
Of an unhappy beauty, a false fair one
Who plighted to a noble youth her faith,
When she had giv'n her honor to a wretch.

CALISTA
Death and confusion! Have I lived to this?
Thus to be treated with unmanly insolence!
To be the sport of a loose ruffian's tongue!
Thus to be used! Thus, like the vilest creature
That ever was a slave to vice and infamy!

HORATIO

By honor and fair truth, you wrong me much,
For on my soul nothing but strong necessity
Could urge my tongue to this ungrateful office;
I came with strong reluctance, as if death
Had stood across my way, to save your honor,
Yours and Sciolto's, yours and Altamont's,
Like one who ventures through a burning pile
To save his tender wife, with all her brood
Of little fondlings, from the dreadful ruin.

CALISTA

Is this, is this the famous friend of Altamont,
For noble worth and deeds of arms renowned?
Is this, this tale-bearing, officious fellow
That watches for intelligence from eyes,
This wretched Argus of a jealous husband,
That fills his easy ears with monstrous tales,
And makes him toss, and rave, and wreak at length
Bloody revenge on his defenseless wife,
Who, guiltless, dies because her fool ran mad?

HORATIO

Alas, this rage is vain, for if your fame
Or peace be worth your care, you must be calm,
And listen to the means are left to save 'em.
'Tis now the lucky minute of your fate;
By me your genius speaks, by me it warns you
Never to see that cursed Lothario more,
Unless you mean to be despised, be shunned
By all your virtuous maids and noble matrons,
Unless you have devoted this rare beauty
To infamy, diseases, prostitution—

CALISTA

Dishonor blast thee, base, unmannered slave,
That dar'st forget my birth and sacred sex,
And shock me with the rude, unhallowed sound!

HORATIO

Here kneel, and in the awful face of heav'n
Breathe out a solemn vow never to see, 160
Nor think, if possible, on him that ruined thee;
Or by my Altamont's dear life I swear,
This paper! —Nay, you must not fly! —This paper,

[Holding her.

This guilty paper shall divulge your shame.

CALISTA
What mean'st thou by that paper?
What contrivance
Hast thou been forging to deceive my father,
To turn his heart against his wretched daughter,
That Altamont and thou may share his wealth?
A wrong like this will make me ev'n forget
The weakness of my sex. O for a sword
To urge my vengeance on the villainous hand
That forged the scroll.

HORATIO
Behold, can this be forged?
See where Calista's name—

[Showing the letter near.

CALISTA
To atoms thus,

[Tearing it.

Thus let me tear the vile, detested falsehood,
The wicked, lying evidence of shame.

HORATIO
Confusion!

CALISTA
Henceforth, thou officious fool,
Meddle no more, nor dare ev'n on thy life
To breathe an accent that may touch my virtue;
I am myself the guardian of my honor,
And wo' not bear so insolent a monitor.

[Enter **ALTAMONT**.

ALTAMONT
Where is my life, my love, my charming bride,
Joy of my heart, and pleasure of my eyes,
Religious hardships will I learn to bear,
To fast, and freeze at midnight hours of pray'r;
Nor think it hard, within a lonely cell,
With melancholy, speechless saints to dwell,
But bless the day I to that refuge ran,

Free from the marriage chain and from that tyrant, man.

[Exit **CALISTA**.

ALTAMONT
She's gone; and as she went, ten thousand fires
Shot from her angry eyes, as if she meant
Too well to keep the cruel vow she made.
Now as thou art a man, Horatio, tell me,
What means this wild confusion in thy looks,
As if thou wert at variance with thyself,
Madness and reason combating within thee,
And thou wert doubtful which should get the better?

HORATIO
I would be dumb forever, but thy fate
Has otherwise decreed it; thou hast seen
That idol of thy soul, that fair Calista,
Thou hast beheld her tears.

ALTAMONT
I have seen her weep,
I have seen that lovely one, that dear Calista,
Complaining in the bitterness of sorrow,
That thou—my friend, Horatio—thou hadst wronged her!

HORATIO
That I have wronged her! Had her eyes been fed
From that rich stream which warms her heart, and numbered
For ev'ry falling tear a drop of blood,
It had not been too much; for she has ruined thee,
Ev'n thee, my Altamont! She has undone thee.

ALTAMONT
Dost thou join ruin with Calista's name?
What is so fair, so exquisitely good?
Is she not more than painting can express,
Or youthful poets fancy, when they love?
Does she not come, like wisdom or good fortune,
Replete with blessings, giving wealth and honor?
The dowry which she brings is peace and pleasure,
And everlasting joys are in her arms.

HORATIO
It had been better thou hadst lived a beggar,
And fed on scraps at great men's surly doors
Than to have matched with one so false, so fatal—

ALTAMONT

It is too much for friendship to allow thee;
Because I tamely bore the wrong thou didst her,
Thou dost avow the barb'rous, brutal part,
And urge the injury ev'n to my face.

HORATIO

I see she has got possession of thy heart,
She has charmed thee, like a siren, to her bed,
With looks of love and with enchanting sounds;
Too late the rocks and quicksands will appear.
When thou art wrecked upon the faithless shore,
Then vainly wish thou hadst not left thy friend
To follow her delusion.

ALTAMONT

If thy friendship
Do churlishly deny my love a room,
It is not worth my keeping; I disclaim it.

HORATIO

Canst thou so soon forget what I've been to thee?
I shared the task of nature with thy father,
And formed with care thy unexperienced youth
To virtue and to arms.
Thy noble father, O thou light young man!
Would he have used me thus? One fortune fed us,
For his was ever mine, mine his, and both
Together flourished, and together fell.
He called me friend, like thee; would he have left me
Thus, for a woman, nay, a vile one too?

ALTAMONT

Thou canst not, dar'st not mean it; speak again,
Say, who is vile? But dare not name Calista.

HORATIO

I had not spoke at first unless compelled,
And forced to clear myself; but since thus urged,
I must avow I do not know a viler.

ALTAMONT

Thou wert my father's friend, he loved thee well;
A kind of venerable mark of him
Hangs round thee, and protects thee from my vengeance;
I cannot, dare not lift my sword against thee,
But henceforth never let me see thee more.

[Going out.

HORATIO
I love thee still, ungrateful as thou art,
And must and will preserve thee from dishonor,
Ev'n in despite of thee.

[Holds him.

ALTAMONT
Let go my arm.

HORATIO
If honor be thy care, if thou wouldst live
Without the name of credulous, wittol husband,
Avoid thy bride, shun her detested bed;
The joys it yields are dashed with poison—

ALTAMONT
Off!
To urge me but a minute more is fatal.

HORATIO
She is polluted! Stained!

ALTAMONT
Madness and raving!
But hence!

HORATIO
Dishonored by the man you hate—

ALTAMONT
I prithee loose me yet, for thy own sake,
If life be worth the keeping—

HORATIO
By Lothario.

ALTAMONT
Perdition take thee, villain, for the falsehood.

[Strikes him.

Now nothing but thy life can make atonement.

HORATIO
A blow! Thou hast used well—

[Draws.

ALTAMONT
This to thy heart—

HORATIO
Yet hold!—By heav'n, his father's in his face.
Spite of my wrongs, my heart runs o'er with tenderness,
And I could rather die myself than hurt him.

ALTAMONT
Defend thyself, for by my much wronged love,
I swear the poor evasion shall not save thee.

HORATIO
Yet hold! Thou know'st I dare!—Think how we've lived—
They fight: Altamont presses on Horatio, who retires.
Nay! Then 'tis brutal violence! And thus,
Thus nature bids me guard the life she gave.

[They fight.

[**LAVINIA** enters, and runs between their swords.

LAVINIA
My brother! My Horatio! Is it possible?
O, turn your cruel swords upon Lavinia!
If you must quench your impious rage in blood,
Behold, my heart shall give you all her store
To save those dearer streams that flow from yours.

ALTAMONT
'Tis well thou hast found a safeguard; none but this,
No pow'r on earth could save thee from my fury.

LAVINIA
O fatal, deadly sound!

HORATIO
Safety from thee!
Away, vain boy! Hast thou forgot the reverence
Due to my arm, thy first, thy great example,
Which pointed out thy way to noble daring,
And showed thee what it was to be a man?

LAVINIA
What busy, meddling fiend, what foe to goodness,

Could kindle such a discord? O, lay by
Those most ungentle looks and angry weapons.
Unless you mean my griefs and killing fears
Should stretch me out at your relentless feet,
A wretched corse, the victim of your fury.

HORATIO

Ask'st thou what made us foes? 'Twas base ingratitude;
'Twas such a sin to friendship as heaven's mercy,
That strives with man's untoward, monstrous wickedness,
Unwearied with forgiving, scarce could pardon.
He who was all to me, child, brother, friend!
With barb'rous, bloody malice sought my life.

ALTAMONT

Thou art my sister, and I would not make thee
The lonely mourner of a widowed bed;
Therefore thy husband's life is safe; but warn him
No more to know this hospitable roof.
He has but ill repaid Sciolto's bounty;
We must not meet; 'tis dangerous. Farewell.
He is going; Lavinia holds him.

LAVINIA

Stay, Altamont, my brother, stay, if ever
Nature or what is nearer much than nature,
The kind consent of our agreeing minds,
Have made us dear to one another, stay,
And speak one gentle word to your Horatio.
Behold, his anger melts, he longs to love you,
To call you friend, then press you hard, with all
The tender, speechless joy of reconcilement.

ALTAMONT

It cannot, sha' not be! You must not hold me.

LAVINIA

Look kindly then!

ALTAMONT

Each minute that I stay
Is a new injury to fair Calista.
From thy false friendship to her arms I'll fly;
There if in any pause of love I rest,
Breathless with bliss, upon her panting breast,
In broken, melting accents I will swear
Henceforth to trust my heart with none but her;
Then own the joys which on her charms attend

Have more than paid me for my faithless friend.

[**ALTAMONT** breaks from **LAVINIA**, and exit.

HORATIO
O, raise thee, my Lavinia, from the earth;
It is too much, this tide of flowing grief,
This wond'rous waste of tears, too much to give
To an ungrateful friend and cruel brother.

LAVINIA
Is there not cause for weeping? O, Horatio!
A brother and a husband were my treasure;
'Twas all the little wealth that poor Lavinia
Saved from the shipwreck of her father's fortunes.
One half is lost already; if thou leav'st me,
If thou shouldst prove unkind to me as Altamont,
Whom shall I find to pity my distress,
To have compassion on a helpless wanderer,
And give her where to lay her wretched head?

HORATIO
Why dost thou wound me with thy soft complainings?
Though Altamont be false and use me hardly,
Yet think not I impute his crimes to thee.
Talk not of being forsaken, for I'll keep thee
Next to my heart, my certain pledge of happiness.
Heav'n formed thee gentle, fair, and full of goodness,
And made thee all my portion here on earth;
It gave thee to me as a large amends
For fortune, friends, and all the world beside.

LAVINIA
Then you will love me still, cherish me ever,
And hide me from misfortune in your bosom:
Here end my cares, nor will I lose one thought
How we shall live or purchase food or raiment.
The holy pow'r, who clothes the senseless earth
With woods, with fruits, with flow'rs and verdant grass,
Whose bounteous hand feeds the whole brute creation,
Knows all our wants and has enough to give us.

HORATIO
From Genoa, from falsehood and inconstancy,
To some more honest, distant clime we'll go;
Nor will I be beholding to my country
For aught but thee, the partner of my flight.

LAVINIA
Yes, I will follow thee, forsake for thee
My country, brother, friends, ev'n all I have;
Though mine's a little all, yet were it more,
And better far, it should be left for thee,
And all that I would keep should be Horatio.
So when the merchant sees his vessel lost,
Though richly freighted from a foreign coast,
Gladly for life the treasure he would give,
And only wishes to escape and live.
Gold and his gains no more employ his mind,
But, driving o'er the billows with the wind,
Cleaves to one faithful plank and leaves the rest behind

[Exeunt.

ACT IV

SCENE I – A Garden

Enter **ALTAMONT.**

ALTAMONT
With what unequal tempers are we formed?
One day the soul, supine with ease and fullness,
Revels secure, and fondly tells herself
The hour of evil can return no more;
The next, the spirits palled, and sick of riot,
Turn all to discord, and we hate our beings,
Curse the past joy, and think it folly all,
And bitterness and anguish. O, last night!
What has ungrateful beauty paid me back
For all that mass of friendship which I squandered?
Coldness, aversion, tears, and sullen sorrow
Dashed all my bliss, and damped my bridal bed.
Soon as the morning dawned, she vanished from me,
Relentless to the gentle call of love.
I have lost a friend, and I have gained—a wife!
Turn not to thought, my brain; but let me find
Some unfrequented shade; there lay me down,
And let forgetful dullness steal upon me
To soften and assuage this pain of thinking.

[Exit.

[Enter **LOTHARIO** and **CALISTA**.

LOTHARIO

Weep not, my fair, but let the god of love
Laugh in thy eyes and revel in thy heart,
Kindle again his torch and hold it high
To light us to new joys; nor let a thought
Of discord or disquiet past, molest thee;
But to a long oblivion give thy cares,
And let us melt the present hour in bliss.

CALISTA

Seek not to soothe me with thy false endearments,
To charm me with thy softness; 'tis in vain;
Thou canst no more betray, nor I be ruined.
The hours of folly and of fond delight
Are wasted all and fled; those that remain
Are doomed to weeping, anguish, and repentance.
I come to charge thee with a long account
Of all the sorrows I have known already,
And all I have to come; thou hast undone me.

LOTHARIO

Unjust Calista! Dost thou call it ruin
To love as we have done: to melt, to languish,
To wish for somewhat exquisitely happy,
And then be blest ev'n to that wish's height?
To die with joy, and straight to live again,
Speechless to gaze, and with tumultuous transport—

CALISTA

O, let me hear no more; I cannot bear it,
'Tis deadly to remembrance; let that night,
That guilty night, be blotted from the year;
Let not the voice of mirth or music know it;
Let it be dark and desolate, no stars
To glitter o'er it; let it wish for light,
Yet want it still, and vainly wait the dawn;
For 'twas the night that gave me up to shame,
To sorrow, to perfidious, false Lothario.

LOTHARIO

Hear this, ye pow'rs, mark how the fair deceiver
Sadly complains of violated truth;
She calls me false, ev'n she, the faithless she,
Whom day and night, whom heav'n and earth have heard
Sighing to vow, and tenderly protest
Ten thousand times, she would be only mine;
And yet, behold, she has giv'n herself away,

Fled from my arms, and wedded to another,
Ev'n to the man whom most I hate on earth—

CALISTA
Art thou so base to upbraid me with a crime
Which nothing but thy cruelty could cause?
If indignation, raging in my soul
For thy unmanly insolence and scorn,
Urged me to do a deed of desperation,
And wound myself to be revenged on thee,
Think whom I should devote to death and hell,
Whom curse as my undoer but Lothario;
Hadst thou been just, not all Sciolto's pow'r,
Not all the vows and pray'rs of sighing Altamont
Could have prevailed, or won me to forsake thee.

LOTHARIO
How have I failed in justice or in love?
Burns not my flame as brightly as at first?
Ev'n now my heart beats high, I languish for thee,
My transports are as fierce, as strong my wishes,
As if thou hadst never blest me with thy beauty.

CALISTA
How didst thou dare to think that I would live
A slave to base desires and brutal pleasures,
To be a wretched wanton for thy leisure,
To toy and waste an hour of idle time with?
My soul disdains thee for so mean a thought.

LOTHARIO
The driving storm of passion will have way,
And I must yield before it; wert thou calm,
Love, the poor criminal whom thou hast doomed,
Has yet a thousand tender things to plead
To charm thy rage and mitigate his fate.

[Enter behind them **ALTAMONT**.

ALTAMONT.
I have lost my peace—Ha! Do I live and wake!

CALISTA
Hadst thou been true, how happy had I been!
Nor Altamont but thou hadst been my lord.
But wherefore named I happiness with thee?
It is for thee, for thee, that I am cursed;
For thee my secret soul each hour arraigns me,

Calls me to answer for my virtue stained,
My honor lost to thee; for thee it haunts me
With stern Sciolto vowing vengeance on me;
With Altamont complaining for his wrongs—

ALTAMONT
Behold him here—

[Coming forward.

CALISTA
Ah—

[Starting.

ALTAMONT
The wretch, whom thou hast made!
Curses and sorrows has thou heaped upon him,
And vengeance is the only good is left.

LOTHARIO
Thou hast ta'en me somewhat unawares, 'tis true,
But love and war take turns like day and night,
And little preparation serves my turn,
Equal to both, and armed for either field.
We've long been foes; this moment ends our quarrel;
Earth, heav'n, and fair Calista judge the combat.

CALISTA
Distraction! Fury! Sorrow! Shame, and death!

ALTAMONT.
Thou hast talked too much; thy breath is poison to me;
It taints the ambient air; this for thy father,
This for Sciolto, and this last for Altamont.

[They fight; **LOTHARIO** is wounded once or twice, and then falls.

LOTHARIO
O, Altamont! Thy genius is the stronger;
Thou hast prevailed! My fierce, ambitious soul,
Declining, droops, and all her fires grow pale;
Yet let not this advantage swell thy pride;
I conquered in my turn; in love I triumphed;
Those joys are lodged beyond the reach of fate;
That sweet revenge comes smiling to my thoughts,
Adorns my fall, and cheers my heart in dying.

[Dies.

CALISTA
And what remains for me? Beset with shame,
Encompassed round with wretchedness, there is
But this one way to break the toil and 'scape.

[She catches up Lothario's sword, and offers to kill herself;

[**ALTAMONT** runs to her, and wrests it from her.

ALTAMONT
What means thy frantic rage?
Off! Let me go.
O, thou hast more than murdered me, yet still,
Still art thou here! And my soul starts with horror
At thought of any danger that may reach thee.

CALISTA
Think'st thou I mean to live, to be forgiven?
O, thou hast known but little of Calista;
If thou hadst never heard my shame, if only
The midnight moon and silent stars had seen it,
I would not bear to be reproached by them,
But dig down deep to find a grave beneath,
And hide me from their beams.

SCIOLTO [within]
What ho, my son!

ALTAMONT
It is Sciolto calls; come near, and find me,
The wretched'st thing of all my kind on earth.

CALISTA
Is it the voice of thunder, or my father?
Madness! Confusion! Let the storm come on,
Let the tumultuous roar drive all upon me,
Dash my devoted bark; ye surges, break it;
'Tis for my ruin that the tempest rises.
When I am lost, sunk to the bottom low,
Peace shall return, and all be calm again.

[Enter **SCIOLTO**.

SCIOLTO
Ev'n now Rossano leaped the garden walls—
Ha! Death has been among you—O my fears!

Last night thou hadst a diff'rence with thy friend;
The cause thou gav'st me for it was a damned one.
Didst thou not wrong the man who told thee truth?
Answer me quick—

ALTAMONT

O, press me not to speak;
Ev'n now my heart is breaking, and the mention
Will lay me dead before you; see that body,
And guess my shame, my ruin! O, Calista!

SCIOLTO

It is enough! But I am slow to execute,
And justice lingers in my lazy hand;
Thus let me wipe dishonor from my name,
And cut thee from the earth, thou stain to goodness.

[Offers to kill **CALISTA**; **ALTAMONT** holds him.

ALTAMONT

Stay thee, Sciolto, thou rash father, stay,
Or turn the point on me, and through my breast
Cut out the bloody passage to Calista;
So shall my love be perfect, while for her
I die, for whom alone I wished to live.

CALISTA

No, Altamont! My heart, that scorned thy love,
Shall never be indebted to thy pity;
Thus torn, defaced, and wretched as I seem,
Still I have something of Sciolto's virtue.
Yes, yes, my father, I applaud thy justice;
Strike home, and I will bless thee for the blow;
Be merciful, and free me from my pain;
'Tis sharp, 'tis terrible, and I could curse
The cheerful day, men, earth, and heav'n, and thee,
Ev'n thee, thou venerable good old man,
For being author of a wretch like me.

ALTAMONT

Listen not to the wildness of her raving.
Remember nature! Should thy daughter's murder
Defile that hand so just, so great in arms,
Her blood would rest upon thee to posterity,
Pollute thy name, and sully all thy wars.

CALISTA

Have I not wronged his gentle nature much?

And yet behold him pleading for my life.
Lost as thou art to virtue, O Calista,
I think thou canst not bear to be outdone;
Then haste to die, and be obliged no more.

SCIOLTO

Thy pious care has giv'n me time to think,
And saved me from a crime; then rest, my sword;
To honor have I kept thee ever sacred,
Nor will I stain thee with a rash revenge;
But mark me well, I will have justice done;
Hope not to bear away thy crimes unpunished;
I will see justice executed on thee,
Ev'n to a Roman strictness; and thou, nature,
Or whatso'er thou art that plead'st within me,
Be still, thy tender strugglings are in vain.

CALISTA

Then am I doomed to live and bear your triumph?
To groan beneath your scorn and fierce upbraidings,
Daily to be reproached, and have my misery
At morn, at noon, and night told over to me,
Lest my remembrance might grow pitiful
And grant a moment's interval of peace;
Is this, is this the mercy of a father?
I only beg to die, and he denies me.

SCIOLTO

Hence from my sight; thy father cannot bear thee;
Fly with thy infamy to some dark cell
Where on the confines of eternal night,
Mourning, misfortune, cares, and anguish dwell;
Where ugly shame hides her opprobrious head,
And death and hell detested rule maintain;
There howl out the remainder of thy life,
And wish thy name may be no more remembered.

CALISTA

Yes, I will fly to some such dismal place,
And be more cursed than you can wish I were;
This fatal form that drew on my undoing,
Fasting and tears and hardship shall destroy;
Nor light nor food nor comfort will I know,
Nor aught that may continue hated life.
Then when you see me meager, wan, and changed,
Stretched at my length, and dying in my cave,
On that cold earth I mean shall be my grave,
Perhaps you may relent and, sighing, say,

At length her tears have washed her stains away,
At length 'tis time her punishment should cease;
Die, thou poor suff'ring wretch, and be at peace.

[Exit **CALISTA**.

SCIOLTO
Who of my servants wait there?

[Enter **TWO** or **THREE SERVANTS**.

On your lives
Take care my doors be guarded well, that none
Pass out or enter but by my appointment.

[Exeunt **SERVANTS**.

ALTAMONT
There is a fatal fury in your visage;
It blazes fierce, and menaces destruction;
My father, I am sick of many sorrows;
Ev'n now my easy heart is breaking with 'em;
Yet, above all, one fear distracts me most:
I tremble at the vengeance which you meditate
On the poor, faithless, lovely, dear Calista.

SCIOLTO
Hast thou not read what brave Virginius did?
With his own hand he slew his only daughter
To save her from the fierce Decemvir's lust.
He slew her yet unspotted to prevent
The shame which she might know.
Then what should I do?
But thou hast tied my hand—I wo' not kill her;
Yet by the ruin she has brought upon us,
The common infamy that brands us both,
She sha' not 'scape.

ALTAMONT
You mean that she shall die then.

SCIOLTO
Ask me not what, nor how, I have resolved,
For all within is anarchy and uproar.
O, Altamont! What a vast scheme of joy
Has this one day destroyed! Well did I hope
This daughter would have blessed my latter days,
That I should live to see you the world's wonder,

So happy, great, and good that none were like you,
While I, from busy life and care set free,
Had spent the evening of my age at home,
Among a little prattling race of yours;
There, like an old man, talked a while, and then
Lain down and slept in peace. Instead of this,
Sorrow and shame must bring me to my grave;
O, damn her, damn her!

[Enter a **SERVANT**.

SERVANT
Arm yourself, my lord;
Rossano, who but now escaped the garden,
Has gathered in the street a band of rioters
Who threaten you and all your friends with ruin
Unless Lothario be returned in safety.

SCIOLTO
By heav'n, their fury rises to my wish,
Nor shall misfortune know my house alone,
But thou, Lothario, and thy race shall pay me
For all the sorrows which my age is cursed with.
I think my name as great, my friends as potent
As any in the state; all shall be summoned;
I know that all will join their hands to ours,
And vindicate thy vengeance. Raise the body,
And bear it in; his friends shall buy him dearly;
I will have blood for ransom; when our force
Is full and armed, we shall expect thy sword
To join with us and sacrifice to justice.

[The body of **LOTHARIO** is carried off by **SERVANTS**.

[Manet **ALTAMONT**.

ALTAMONT
There is a stupid weight upon my senses,
A dismal, sullen stillness that succeeds
The storm of rage and grief, like silent death
After the tumult and the noise of life.
Would it were death, as sure 'tis wond'rous like it,
For I am sick of living, my soul's palled;
She kindles not with anger or revenge;
Love was th'informing, active fire within;
Now that is quenched, the mass forgets to move,
And longs to mingle with its kindred earth.

[A tumultuous noise with clashing of swords, as at a little distance.

[Enter **LAVINIA** with **TWO SERVANTS**, their swords drawn.

LAVINIA
Fly, swiftly fly to my Horatio's aid,
Nor lose you vain, officious cares on me;
Bring me my lord, my husband to my arms;
He is Lavinia's life; bring him me safe,
And I shall be at ease, be well and happy.

ALTAMONT
Art thou Lavinia? O, what barb'rous hand
Could wring thy poor, defenseless innocence
And leave such marks of more than savage fury?

LAVINIA
My brother! O, my heart is full of fears;
Perhaps ev'n now my dear Horatio bleeds.
Not far from hence, as passing to the port,
By a mad multitude we were surrounded,
Who ran upon us with uplifted swords
And cried aloud for vengeance and Lothario.
My lord with ready boldness stood the shock
To shelter me from danger, but in vain,
Had not a party from Sciolto's palace
Rushed out and snatched me from amidst the fray.

ALTAMONT
What of my friend?

LAVINIA [looking out]
Ha! By my joys, 'tis he;
He lives, he comes to bless me, he is safe!

[Enter **HORATIO** with **TWO** or **THREE SERVANTS**, their swords drawn.

FIRST SERVANT
'Twere at the utmost hazard of your life
To venture forth again till we are stronger;
Their number trebles ours.

HORATIO
No matter, let it;
Death is not half so shocking as that traitor.
My honest soul is mad with indignation
To think her plainness could be so abused
As to mistake that wretch and call him friend;

I cannot bear the sight.

ALTAMONT
Open, thou earth,
Gape wide, and take me down to thy dark bosom
To hide me from Horatio.

HORATIO
O, Lavinia,
Believe not but I joy to see thee safe.
Would our ill fortune had not drove us hither;
I could ev'n wish we rather had been wrecked
On any other shore than saved on this.

LAVINIA
O, let us bless the mercy that preserved us,
That gracious pow'r that saved us for each other,
And, to adorn the sacrifice of praise,
Offer forgiveness too; be thou like heav'n,
And put away th'offenses of thy friend
Far, far from thy remembrance.

ALTAMONT
I have marked him
To see if one forgiving glance stole hither,
If any spark of friendship were alive
That would by sympathy at meeting glow,
And strive to kindle up the flame anew;
'Tis lost, 'tis gone, his soul is quite estranged,
And knows me for its counterpart no more.

HORATIO
Thou know'st thy rule, thy empire in Horatio,
Nor canst thou ask in vain, command in vain
Where nature, reason, nay, where love is judge;
But when you urge my temper to comply
With what it most abhors, I cannot do it.

LAVINIA
Where didst thou get this sullen, gloomy hate?
It was not in thy nature to be thus;
Come, put if off, and let thy heart be cheerful,
Be gay again, and know the joys of friendship,
The trust, security, and mutual tenderness,
The double joys, where each is glad for both;
Friendship, the wealth, the last retreat and strength,
Secure against ill fortune and the world.

HORATIO
I am not apt to take a light offense,
But patient of the failings of my friends,
And willing to forgive; but when an injury
Stabs to the heart and rouses my resentment
(Perhaps it is the fault of my rude nature),
I own I cannot easily forget it.

ALTAMONT
Thou hast forgot me.

HORATIO
No.

ALTAMONT
Why are thy eyes
Impatient of me then, scornful and fierce?

HORATIO
Because they speak the meaning of my heart;
Because they are honest and disdain a villain.

ALTAMONT
I have wronged thee much, Horatio.

HORATIO
True, thou hast;
When I forget it, may I be a wretch
Vile as thyself, a false, perfidious fellow,
An infamous, believing, British husband.

ALTAMONT
I've wronged thee much, and heav'n has well avenged it.
I have not, since we parted, been at peace,
Nor known one joy sincere; our broken friendship
Pursued me to the last retreat of love,
Stood glaring like a ghost, and made me cold with horror.
Misfortunes on misfortunes press upon me,
Swell o'er my head like waves, and dash me down.
Sorrow, remorse, and shame have torn my soul;
They hang like winter on my youthful hopes,
And blast the spring and promise of my year.

LAVINIA
So flow'rs are gathered to adorn a grave,
To lose their freshness amongst bones and rottenness,
And have their odors stifled in the dust.
Canst thou hear this, thou cruel, hard Horatio?

Canst thou behold thy Altamont undone?
That gentle, that dear youth! Canst thou behold him,
His poor heart broken, death in his pale visage,
And groaning out his woes, yet stand unmoved?

HORATIO
The brave and wise I pity in misfortune,
But when ingratitude and folly suffers,
'Tis weakness to be touched.

ALTAMONT
I wo' not ask thee
To pity or forgive me, but confess
This scorn, this insolence of hate is just;
'Tis constancy of mind and manly in thee.
But, O, had I been wronged by thee, Horatio,
There is a yielding softness in my heart
Could ne'er have stood it out, but I had ran
With streaming eyes and open arms upon thee,
And pressed thee close, close!

HORATIO
I must hear no more;
The weakness is contagious; I shall catch it,
And be a tame, fond wretch.

LAVINIA
Where wouldst thou go?
Wouldst thou part thus? You sha' not, 'tis impossible;
For I will bar thy passage, kneeling thus;
Perhaps thy cruel hand may spurn me off,
But I will throw my body in thy way,
And thou shalt trample o'er my faithful bosom,
Tread on me, wound me, kill me ere thou pass.

ALTAMONT
Urge not in vain thy pious suit, Lavinia;
I have enough to rid me of my pain.
Calista, thou hadst reached my heart before;
To make all sure, my friend repeats the blow.
But in the grave our cares shall be forgotten;
There love and friendship cease.

[**LAVINIA** runs to him, and endeavors to raise him.

LAVINIA
Speak to me, Altamont.
He faints! He dies! Now turn and see thy triumph,

My brother! But our cares shall end together;
Here will I lay me down by thy dear side,
Bemoan thy too hard fate, then share it with thee,
And never see my cruel lord again.
Horatio runs to Altamont, and raises him in his arms.

HORATIO
It is too much to bear! Look up, my Altamont!
My stubborn, unrelenting heart has killed him.
Look up and bless me, tell me that thou liv'st.
O, I have urged they gentleness too far; He revives.
Do thou and my Lavinia both forgive me;
A flood of tenderness comes o'er my soul;
I cannot speak! I love, forgive, and pity thee!

ALTAMONT
I thought that nothing could have stayed my soul,
That long ere this her flight had reached the stars;
But thy known voice has lured her back again.
Methinks I fain would set all right with thee,
Make up this most unlucky breach, and then,
With thine and heav'n's forgiveness on my soul,
Shrink to my grave, and be at ease forever.

HORATIO
By heav'n, my heart bleeds for thee; ev'n this moment
I feel thy pangs of disappointed love.
Is it not pity that this youth should fail,
That all this wond'rous goodness should be lost,
And the world never know it? O, my Altamont!
Give me thy sorrows, let me bear 'em for thee,
And shelter thee from ruin.

LAVINIA
O, my brother!
Think not but we will share in all thy woes;
We'll sit all day and tell sad tales of love,
And when we light upon some faithless woman,
Some beauty, like Calista, false and fair,
We'll fix our grief and our complaining there;
We'll curse the nymph that drew the ruin on,
And mourn the youth that was like thee undone.

[Exeunt.

ACT V

SCENE I

A room hung with black: on one side, **LOTHARIO'S BODY** on a bier; on the other, a table with a skull and other bones, a book, and a lamp on it. **CALISTA** is discovered on a couch in black, her hair hanging loose and dis-ordered; after music and a song, she rises and comes forward.

SONG

I
Hear, you midnight phantoms, hear,
You who pale and wan appear,
And fill the wretch, who wakes, with fear
You who wander, scream, and groan,
Round the mansions once your own,
You whom still your crimes upbraid,
You who rest not with the dead;
From the coverts where you stray,
Where you lurk and shun the day,
From the charnel and the tomb,
Hither haste ye, hither come.

II
Chide Calista for delay,
"I Tell her 'tis for her you stay;
Bid her die and come away.
See the sexton with his spade,
See the grave already made;
Listen, fair one, to thy knell,
This music is thy passing bell.

CALISTA
'Tis well! These solemn sounds, this pomp of horror
Are fit to feed the frenzy in my soul;
Here's room for meditation, ev'n to madness,
Till the mind burst with thinking; this dull flame
Sleeps in the socket; sure the book was left
To tell me something—for inspiration then—
He teaches holy sorrow and contrition
And penitence— Is it become an art then?
A trick that lazy, dull, luxurious gown-men
Can teach us to do over? I'll no more on't;

[Throwing away the book.

I have more real anguish in my heart
Than all their pedant discipline e'er knew.
What charnel has been rifled for these bones?
Fie! This is pageantry—they look uncouthly,

But what of that? If he or she that owned 'em
Safe from disquiet sit, and smile to see
The farce their miserable relics play.
But here's a sight is terrible indeed;
Is this that haughty, gallant, gay Lothario?
That dear perfidious— Ah! how pale he looks!
How grim with clotted blood and those dead eyes!
Ascend, ye ghosts, fantastic forms of night,
In all your diff'rent, dreadful shapes ascend,
And match the present horror if you can.

[Enter **SCIOLTO**.

SCIOLTO.
This dead of night, this silent hour of darkness
Nature for rest ordained and soft repose,
And yet distraction and tumultuous jars
Keep all our frighted citizens awake;
The senate, weak, divided, and irresolute,
Want pow'r to succor the afflicted state.
Vainly in words and long debates they're wise,
While the fierce factions scorn their peaceful orders,
And drown the voice of law in noise and anarchy.
Amidst the general wreck, see where she stands,

[Pointing to **CALISTA**.

Like Helen in the night when Troy was sacked,
Spectatress of the mischief which she made.

CALISTA
It is Sciolto! Be thyself, my soul;
Be strong to bear his fatal indignation,
That he may see thou art not lost so far
But somewhat still of his great spirit lives
In the forlorn Calista.

SCIOLTO
Thou wert once
My daughter.

CALISTA
Happy were it I had died,
And never lost that name.

SCIOLTO
That's something yet;
Thou wert the very darling of my age;

I thought the day too short to gaze upon thee,
That all the blessings I could gather for thee
By cares on earth and by my pray'rs to heav'n
Were little for my fondness to bestow;
Why didst thou turn to folly, then, and curse me?

CALISTA

Because my soul was rudely drawn from yours,
A poor, imperfect copy of my father,
Where goodness and the strength of manly virtue
Was thinly planted, and the idle void
Filled up with light belief and easy fondness;
It was because I loved, and was a woman.

SCIOLTO

Hadst thou been honest, thou hadst been a cherubin;
But of that joy, as of a gem long lost,
Beyond redemption gone, think we no more.
Hast thou e'er dared to meditate on death?

CALISTA

I have, as on the end of shame and sorrow.

SCIOLTO

Ha! Answer me! Say, has thou coolly thought?
'Tis not the stoic's lessons got by rote,
The pomp of words, and pedant dissertations
That can sustain thee in that hour of terror;
Books have taught cowards to talk nobly of it,
But when the trial comes, they start and stand aghast.
Hast thou considered what may happen after it?
How thy account may stand, and what to answer?

CALISTA

I have turned my eyes inward upon myself,
Where foul offense and shame have laid all waste;
Therefore my soul abhors the wretched dwelling,
And longs to find some better place of rest.

SCIOLTO

'Tis justly thought, and worthy of that spirit
That dwelt in ancient Latian breasts when Rome
Was mistress of the world. I would go on
And tell thee all my purpose, but it sticks
Here at my heart, and cannot find a way.

CALISTA

Then spare the telling, if it be a pain,

And write the meaning with your poniard here.

SCIOLTO
O, truly guessed—seest thou this trembling hand—

[Holding up a dagger.

Thrice justice urged—and thrice the slack'ning sinews
Forgot their office and confessed the father;
At length the stubborn virtue has prevailed;
It must, it must be so— O, take it then,

[Giving the dagger.

And know the rest untaught.

CALISTA
I understand you;
It is but thus, and both are satisfied.

[She offers to kill herself; **SCIOLTO** catches hold of her arm.

SCIOLTO
A moment, give me yet a moment's space;
The stern, the rigid judge has been obeyed;
Now nature and the father claim their turns;
I have held the balance with an iron hand,
And put off ev'ry tender, human thought,
To doom my child to death; but spare my eyes
The most unnatural sight, lest their strings crack,
And my old brain split and grow mad with horror.

CALISTA
Ha! Is is possible? And is there yet
Some little, dear remain of love and tenderness
For poor, undone Calista in your heart?

SCIOLTO
O, when I think what pleasure I took in thee,
What joys thou gav'st me in thy prattling infancy,
Thy sprightly wit and early blooming beauty,
How I have stood and fed my eyes upon thee,
Then lifted up my hands and, wond'ring, blessed thee;
By my strong grief, my heart ev'n melts within me;
I could curse nature and that tyrant, honor,
For making me thy father and thy judge;
Thou art my daughter still.

CALISTA

For that kind word
Thus let me fall, thus humbly to the earth,
Weep on your feet, and bless you for this goodness;
O, 'tis too much for this offending wretch,
This parricide, that murders with her crimes,
Shortens her father's age, and cuts him off
Ere little more than half his years be numbered.

SCIOLTO

Would it were otherwise! But thou must die—

CALISTA

That I must die, it is my only comfort;
Death is the privilege of human nature,
And life without it were not worth our taking;
Thither the poor, the pris'ner, and the mourner
Fly for relief and lay their burdens down.
Come then, and take me now to thy cold arms,
Thou meager shade; here let me breathe my last,
Charmed with my father's pity and forgiveness
More than if angels tuned their golden viols,
And sung a requiem to my parting soul.

SCIOLTO

I am summoned hence; ere this my friends expect me;
There is I know not what of sad presage
That tells me I shall never see thee more;
If it be so, this is our last farewell,
And these the parting pangs which nature feels
When anguish rends the heartstrings—O, my daughter!

[Exit **SCIOLTO**.

CALISTA

Now think thou, cursed Calista, now behold
The desolation, horror, blood, and ruin
Thy crimes and fatal folly spread around
That loudly cry for vengeance on thy head;
Yet heav'n, who knows our weak, imperfect natures,
How blind with passions and how prone to evil,
Makes not too strict enquiry for offenses,
But is atoned by penitence and pray'r.
Cheap recompense! Here 'twould not be received;
Nothing but blood can make the expiation,
And cleanse the soul from inbred, deep pollution.
And see, another injured wretch is come
To call for justice from my tardy hand.

[Enter **ALTAMONT**.

ALTAMONT
Hail to you horrors! Hail, thou house of death!
And thou, the lovely mistress of these shades,
Whose beauty gilds the more than midnight darkness,
And makes it grateful as the dawn of day.
O, take me in, a fellow-mourner with thee;
I'll number groan for groan and tear for tear;
And when the fountains of thy eyes are dry,
Mine shall supply the stream and weep for both.

CALISTA
I know thee well; thou art the injured Altamont;
Thou com'st to urge me with the wrongs I ha' done thee;
But know I stand upon the brink of life,
And in a moment mean to set me free
From shame and thy upbraiding.

ALTAMONT
Falsely, falsely
Dost thou accuse me. When did I complain
Or murmur at my fate? For thee I have
Forgot the temper of Italian husbands,
And fondness has prevailed upon revenge;
I bore my load of infamy with patience,
As holy men do punishments from heav'n,
Nor thought it hard, because it came from thee;
O, then forbid me not to mourn thy loss,
To wish some better fate had ruled our loves,
And that Calista had been mine, and true.

CALISTA
O, Altamont, 'tis hard for souls like mine,
Haughty and fierce, to yield they have done amiss;
But, O, behold my proud, disdainful heart
Bends to thy gentler virtue; yes, I own,
Such is thy truth, thy tenderness and love,
Such are the graces that adorn thy youth,
That were I not abandoned to destruction,
With thee I might have lived for ages blest,
And died in peace within thy faithful arms.

ALTAMONT
Then happiness is still within our reach;
Here let remembrance lose our past misfortunes,
Tear all records that hold the fatal story;

Here let our joys begin, from hence go on
In long successive order.

CALISTA
What! In death?

ALTAMONT
Then art thou fixed to die? But be it so,
We'll go together; my advent'rous love
Shall follow thee to those uncertain beings;
Whether our lifeless shades are doomed to wander
In gloomy groves with discontented ghosts,
Or whether through the upper air we fleet,
And tread the fields of light, still I'll pursue thee
Till fate ordains that we shall part no more.

CALISTA
O, no! Heav'n has some better lot in store
To crown thee with; live and be happy long;
Live for some maid that shall deserve thy goodness,
Some kind, unpracticed heart that never yet
Has listened to the false ones of thy sex,
Nor known the arts of ours; she shall reward thee,
Meet thee with virtues equal to thy own,
Charm thee with sweetness, beauty, and with truth,
Be blest in thee alone, and thou in her.

[Enter **HORATIO**.

HORATIO
Now mourn indeed, ye miserable pair,
For now the measure of your woes is full.

ALTAMONT
What dost thou mean, Horatio?

HORATIO
The great, the good Sciolto dies this moment.

CALISTA
My father!

ALTAMONT
That's a deadly stroke indeed.

HORATIO
Not long ago he privately went forth,
Attended but by few, and those unbidden;

I heard which way he took, and straight pursued him,
But found him compassed by Lothario's faction,
Almost alone amidst a crowd of foes;
Too late we brought him aid and drove them back;
Ere that his frantic valor had provoked
The death he seemed to wish for from their swords.

CALISTA
And dost thou bear me yet, thou patient earth?
Dost thou not labor with my murd'rous weight?
And you, ye glitt'ring, heav'nly host of stars,
Hide your fair heads in clouds, or I shall blast you,
For I am all contagion, death, and ruin,
And nature sickens at me; rest, thou world,
This parricide shall be thy plague no more;
Thus, thus I set thee free.

[Stabs herself.

HORATIO
O fatal rashness!

ALTAMONT
Thou dost instruct me well; to length life
Is but to trifle now.

[**ALTAMONT** offers to kill himself; **HORATIO** prevents him, and wrests his sword from him.

HORATIO
Ha! What means
The frantic Altamont?
Some foe to man
Has breathed on ev'ry breast contagious fury
And epidemic madness.

[Enter **SCIOLTO**, pale and bloody, supported by **SERVANTS**.

CALISTA
O my heart!
Well may'st thou fail, for see, the spring that fed
Thy vital stream is wasted and runs low.
My father! Will you now at last forgive me,
If after all my crimes and all your sufferings
I call you once again by that dear name?
Will you forget my shame and those wide wounds,
Lift up your hand, and bless me ere I go
Down to my dark abode?

SCIOLTO

Alas, my daughter!
Thou hast rashly ventured in a stormy sea,
Where life, fame, virtue, all were wrecked and lost;
But sure thou hast borne thy part in all the anguish,
And smarted with the pain; then rest in peace;
Let silence and oblivion hide thy name,
And save thee from the malice of posterity;
And may'st thou find with heav'n the same forgiveness
As with thy father here. Die, and be happy.

CALISTA

Celestial sounds! Peace dawns upon my soul,
And ev'ry pain grows less. —O gentle Altamont,
Think not too hardly of me when I'm gone,
But pity me. Had I but early known
Thy wond'rous worth, thou excellent young man,
We had been happier both. Now 'tis too late,
And yet my eyes take pleasure to behold thee;
Thou wert their last dear object.—Mercy, heav'n!

ALTAMONT

Cold! Dead and cold! And yet thou art not changed,
But lovely still! Hadst thou a thousand faults,
What heart so hard, what virtue so severe
But at that beauty must of force relented,
Melted to pity, love, and to forgiveness?

SCIOLTO

O, turn thee from the fatal object; Altamont,
Come near, and let me bless thee ere I die.
To thee and brave Horatio I bequeath
My fortunes. Lay me by thy noble father,
And love my memory as thou hast done his,
For thou hast been my son.—O gracious heav'n!
Thou that hast endless blessings still in store
For virtue and for filial piety,
Let grief, disgrace, and want be far away,
But multiply thy mercies on his head;
Let honor, greatness, goodness still be with him,
And peace in all his ways.

[He dies.

ALTAMONT

Take, take it all;
To thee, Horatio, I resign the gift
While I pursue my father and my love

And find my only portion in the grave.

[He faints.

HORATIO
The storm of grief bears hard upon his youth,
And bends him like a drooping flower to earth.
Raise him, and bear him in.

[**ALTAMONT** is carried off.

By such examples are we taught to prove
The sorrows that attend unlawful love;
Death or some worse misfortunes soon divide
The injured bridegroom from his guilty bride;
If you would have the nuptial union last,
Let virtue be the bond that ties it fast.

[Exeunt **OMNES**.

EPILOGUE

Spoken by Mrs. Bracegirdle, who played Lavinia

You see the tripping dame could find no favor;
Dearly she paid for breach of good behavior,
Nor could her loving husband's fondness save her.
Italian ladies lead but scurvy lives;
There's dreadful dealing with eloping wives;
Thus 'tis because these husbands are obeyed
By force of laws which for themselves they made.
With tales of old prescriptions they confine "
The right of marriage-rule to their male line,
And huff and domineer by right divine.
Had we the pow'r, we'd make the tyrants know
What 'tis to fail in duties which they owe;
We'd teach the saunt'ring squire who loves to roam,
Forgetful of his own dear spouse and home,
Who snores at night supinely by her side,
'Twas not for this the nuptial knot was tied.
The plodding pettifogger and the cit
Have learned at least this modern way of wit:
Each ill-bred, senseless rogue, though ne'er so dull,
Has th' impudence to think his wife a fool;
He spends the night where merry wags resort,
With joking clubs and eighteen-penny port,

While she, poor soul, 's contented to regale
By a sad sea-coal fire with wigs and ale.
Well may the cuckold-making tribe find grace,
And fill an absent husband's empty place;
If you would e'er bring constancy in fashion,
You men must first begin the reformation.
Then shall the golden age of love return,
No turtle for her wand'ring mate shall mourn,
No foreign charms shall cause domestic strife,
But ev'ry married man shall toast his wife;
Phyllis shall not be to the country sent,
For carnivals in town to keep a tedious Lent;
Lampoons shall cease, and envious scandal die,
And all shall live in peace, like my good man and I.

Nicholas Rowe – A Concise Bibliography

Poems
A Poem upon the Late Glorious Successes of Her Majesty's Arms (1707)
Poems on Several Occasions (1714)
Maecenas. Verses occasion'd by the honours conferr'd on the Right Honourable Earl of Halifax (1714)
Ode for the New Year MDCCXVI (1716)

Original Plays
The Ambitious Stepmother (1700)
Tamerlane (1702)
The Biter (1705)
Ulysses (1705)
The Royal Convert (1707)
The Tragedy of Jane Shore (1714)
Lady Jane Grey (1715)

Adaptations and Translations
The Fair Penitent (1702/3), an adaptation of Massinger and Field's The Fatal Dowry
Lucan (1718), a paraphrase of the Pharsalia
Callipaedia (date unknown), translation of Claude Quillet

Edited Works
The Works of William Shakespear (London: Jacob Tonson, 1709), first modern edition of the plays.

Miscellaneous Works
Memoir of Boileau (date unknown), prefixed to translation of Lutrin
Some Account of the Life of Mr. William Shakespear

www.ingramcontent.com/pod-product-compliance
Lightning Source LLC
Chambersburg PA
CBHW060051050426
42448CB00011B/2402